HOW DOES
IT GROW?

FROG

by Jinny Johnson
Illustrations by Graham Rosewarne

A+
Smart Apple Media
Rocky River Public Library

Smart Apple Media
P.O. Box 3263, Mankato, MN 56002

Printed in the United States of America

Library of Congress Cataloging-in-Publication Data

Johnson, Jinny.
  Frog / Jinny Johnson ; illustrations by Graham Rosewarne.
     p. cm. -- (How does it grow?)
  Includes index.
  ISBN 978-1-59920-355-3 (hardcover)
  1. Frogs--Life cycles--Juvenile literature. I. Rosewarne, Graham, ill. II. Title.
  QL668.E2J54 2010
  597.8'9156--dc22

                                                2008053341

All words in **bold** can be found in the glossary on page 30.

Designed by Helen James
Edited by Mary-Jane Wilkins
Picture research by Su Alexander

Photograph acknowledgements
page 5 Keith Ringland/Photolibrary Group; 17 David M Dennis/
Photolibrary Group; 19 Paul Franklin/Photolibrary Group;
29 Michael Leach/Photolibrary Group
Front cover Paul Franklin/Photolibrary Group

9 8 7 6 5 4 3 2 1

Contents

Laying Eggs

Frogs are very happy living on land or in water. But every frog's life starts in water.

A mother frog lays her eggs, sometimes hundreds of them, in a pond. The eggs are inside clumps of clear jelly that help keep them safe. Other animals like to eat frog eggs.

The frog eggs are called **frog spawn**. Can you see the little black specks in the jelly? These are the beginnings of baby frogs.

THE MOTHER FROG SWIMS
AROUND HER FROG SPAWN.

What does the baby frog look like?

A Tiny Tadpole

At first a baby frog looks nothing like its parents. It hatches as a tiny swimming creature called a **tadpole**. A tadpole has a round body and a long tail.

When the tadpoles hatch, they eat the jelly around them. They are small and weak at first and stay together, clinging to water plants.

Tadpoles have feathery strands on their heads called **gills**. Gills help the tadpoles breathe in water.

THE FEATHERY GILLS HELP THE TADPOLES BREATHE.

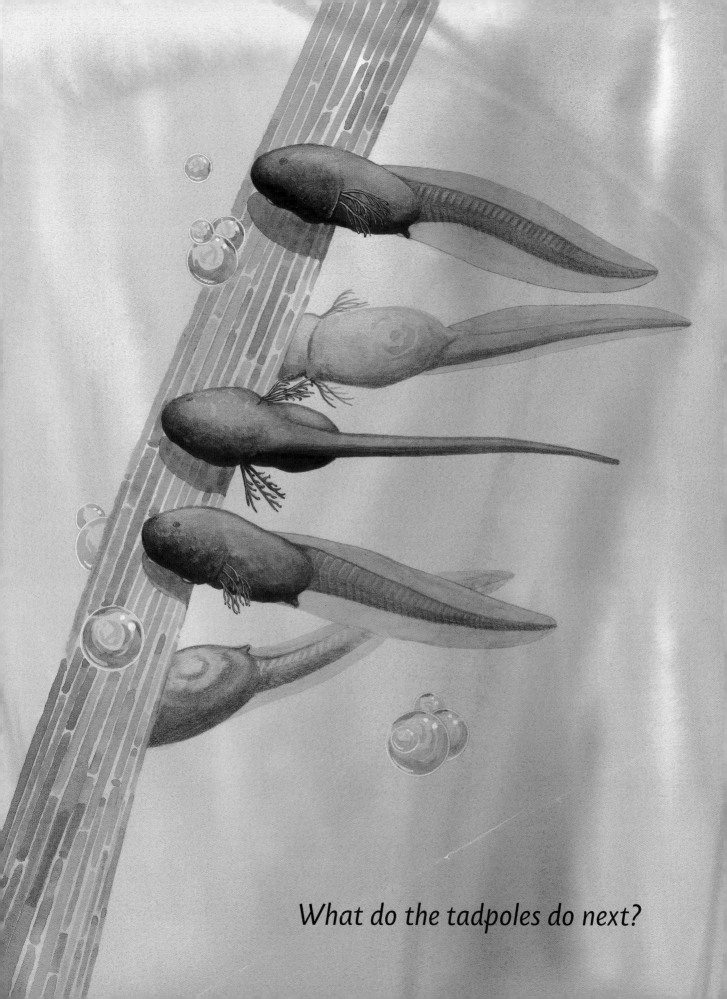

What do the tadpoles do next?

Getting Bigger

A week or so after hatching,
the tadpoles have grown bigger.
They swim around with the help
of their long tails, and they feed
on water plants and other tiny
bits of food.

Fish and birds hunt and eat lots
of tadpoles, but some tadpoles
stay safe and survive.

Gradually the tadpole's feathery
gills disappear, and its **lungs** start
to grow. It comes to the surface
of the water to breathe.

This tadpole takes cover
from a hungry fish.

When does the tadpole grow legs?

Growing Legs

The tadpole's legs begin
to grow when it is between
six and nine weeks old.

The back legs grow first and
the tail starts to get smaller.

You can see bulges on the
tadpole's body where the
front legs will grow.

NOW THE TADPOLE
IS BEGINNING TO
LOOK MORE LIKE
A FROG.

When will the frog grow front legs?

Becoming a Frog

By the time it is eleven weeks old, the tadpole has grown front legs and back legs.

Its tail is starting to disappear. The young frog looks more like a tiny version of its mom.

Now it catches insects to eat,as well as eating plants. Soon it will be able to leave the water.

THE TADPOLE NOW HAS FOUR LEGS.

How will the little frog move on land?

On to Dry Land

Now that the **froglet** has grown bigger, it can hop about on land. Its tail has gone and its legs are growing stronger.

The frog's back legs are much longer than its front ones and help the frog jump into the air.

The frog is big enough to catch many kinds of food. It likes to eat snails, slugs, and worms, as well as insects.

THIS FROG IS WAITING TO JUMP AND CATCH ITS NEXT MEAL.

How does a frog catch its food?

Catching a Meal

A frog catches food with its long
sticky tongue.

Frogs can see well with their big
bulging eyes. When a frog spots
its **prey**, it goes as close as it can.

It jumps toward the prey and flicks
out its long tongue. The sticky tip
of the tongue traps the prey and
whisks it into the frog's mouth in
the blink of an eye.

THIS FROG IS
GOBBLING UP
A GRASSHOPPER.

Can frogs swim as well as jump?

Swimming and Diving

Frogs are good swimmers. Their feet have skin between the toes that helps them paddle along. They are called **webbed feet**.

Frogs spend lots of time on land but like to stay near water. They can dive into the water to escape from animals such as hungry birds.

A FROG HAS FOUR
TOES ON ITS FRONT
FEET AND FIVE ON
ITS BACK FEET.

Why else do frogs like to stay near water?

A Frog's Skin

Frogs like to be near water to keep their skin damp. Frogs "drink" through their skin. The frog's skin lets water in and out. Frogs can breathe through their skin when in water and through their lungs when on land.

Frogs have to sit in the sun to keep their bodies warm. To cool down, they hide in a shady spot. Many frogs can make their skin lighter or darker to help them soak up more or less heat.

FROGS USE NEARBY PLANTS FOR SHADE.

When do frogs have
young of their own?

Calling to a Mate

When a female frog is two or three years old, it starts to look for a mate so it can lay eggs.

Male frogs croak to let female frogs know they are around. Sacs of skin under the chin fill with air when the frog calls. This helps to make the croaking sound louder.

A FROG SITS UNDER THE REEDS AND CROAKS FOR A MATE.

Do females croak too?

Female Frogs

Female frogs don't usually croak,
but they can hear the male's songs.
A female frog knows which calls
are from frogs of her own kind.

Frogs' ears are flat and round.
You can see them on either side
of the frog's head.

FROGS OFTEN
CALL TO THEIR
MATES AT NIGHT.

What happens when a frog lays eggs?

Starting Again

When the female frog is ready to lay her eggs, she goes in the water.

Her mate holds on to her as she lays the eggs. He **fertilizes** the eggs in the water.

Within a day and a half, the eggs will hatch and lots of tadpoles will be swimming in the water. Soon they will grow into frogs.

A FEMALE FROG LAYS HUNDREDS OF EGGS.

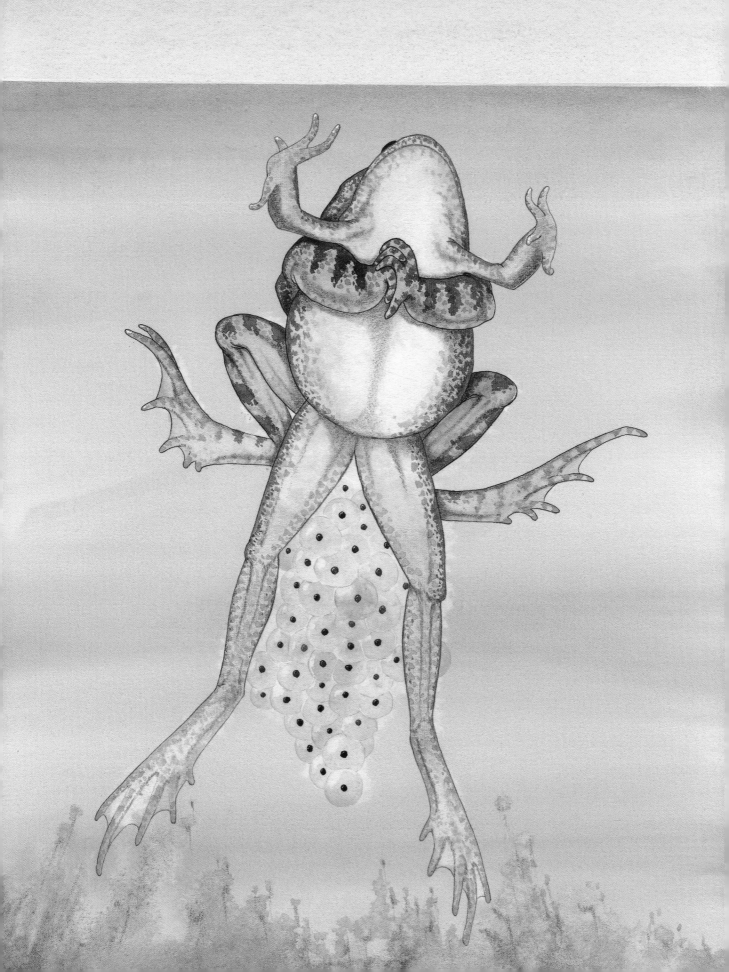

More About Frogs

What is an amphibian?

A frog belongs to a group of animals called **amphibians**. Amphibians evolved from fish and can live on land and in water. Other types of amphibians include toads, newts, and wormlike creatures called caecilians. Frogs have long back legs, webbed feet, and no tail.

Where do frogs live?

There are more than 4,000 kinds of frogs. They live all over the world except in Antarctica. The green frog and the bullfrog are common in North America. Many kinds of frogs are becoming rare because of pollution, climate change, and the destruction of the places where they live.

How big is a frog?

Green frogs can be up to 4 inches (10 cm) long. The bullfrog is much bigger—up to 8 inches (20 cm) long.

THE FROG IS A
POWERFUL JUMPER.

Words to Remember

amphibian
an animal such as a frog or toad that can live
on land and in water

fertilize
A male frog fertilizes eggs by releasing his sperm
in the water with the eggs. A fertilized egg can
grow into a frog.

froglet
a young frog that has recently changed from
a tadpole

frog spawn
a frog's eggs

gills
parts of the body that help an animal breathe in water

lungs
a part of the body used for breathing air

prey
an animal that is hunted and eaten by another animal.

tadpole
the first stage of the life of a frog

webbed feet
feet with flaps of skin between the toes that help
the frog move in water

Web Sites

For Students
Frogland—All About Frogs
http://allaboutfrogs.org/

Images of the Common Frog
http://www.arkive.org/common-frog/rana-temporaria/images.html

For Teachers
Animal Diversity Web
http://animaldiversity.ummz.umich.edu/site/index.html

Frog Exploratorium: Resources for Teachers
http://www.exploratorium.edu/lc/pathfinders/frogs/index.html

Origami Jumping Frog Craft
http://www.enchantedlearning.com/crafts/origami/frog/

Index